DEALING WITH CRIME BY ILLEGAL IMMIGRANTS AND THE OPIOID CRISIS

What to Do about the Two Big Social and Criminal Justice Issues of Today

by Paul Brakke

Author of 6 Books on Criminal Justice and Social Issues in America, including: *Fixing the U.S. Criminal Justice System, the Costly U.S. Prison System,* and *The Great National Divides*

DEALING WITH CRIME BY ILLEGAL IMMIGRANTS AND THE DEATH PENALTY

Copyright 2018 Paul Brakke

TABLE OF CONTENTS

Introduction

Dealing with Crime by Illegal Immigrants and the Opioid Crisis is based on a series of blogs I began writing for the website of my company American Leadership Books (www.americanleadershipbooks.com). I have collected the series into this book.

These blogs were inspired by reading about the immigration and opioid crises in the news. These stories also discussed the various executive orders, efforts to pass legislation, and judicial decisions about the results of the programs that were enacted.

I was especially inspired to write this because for the most part, the news stories in the mainstream media have been opposed to any legislation to crack down on illegal immigration or about efforts to impose the death penalty for drug dealers. For example, many of the stories in the media have featured illegal immigrants who have made a successful life by getting married, having children, and creating a business in the United States, although they have had some convictions for crimes in the distant past. The emphasis has been on the way in which they have been wrenched from their families and communities to return to a homeland where they know no one, apart from a few distant relatives, and may not even speak the language. So these stories highlight the cruelty of these seemingly draconian laws in disrupting the families of these illegal immigrants.

However, while some of these illegal immigrants have turned their lives around, these stories miss the larger picture of having many thousands of illegal immigrants who are involved in crimes. In addition, many now established illegal immigrants did commit serious crimes in the past, which qualifies them for being deported now. Then, too, it is important to look on harsh policies as a deterrent to other individuals who might want to immigrate illegally to the United States. Recognizing the potential for being discovered and deported might lead them to stay home rather than try to sneak into the United States through an easy to access border.

Thus, the other side of the story showing the extent of illegal immigration and the dangers posed by the many illegal immigrants who commit crimes has been missing.

By the same token, much of the media have emphasized the cruelty of the death penalty and urged getting rid of it. But there are some crimes that are so horrendous and truly evil, such as the rash of serial killings committed just for the thrill of it, that the perpetrator should pay the ultimate price. Moreover, it seems like an appropriate penalty for a high level drug dealer who is responsible for thousands of deaths due to drug overdoses, as well as for the many killings associated with dealing drugs, such as in battles over turf. But again, this has been a missing piece of the death penalty controversy.

I have also combined these blogs into a single book, since there is a connection with the illegal immigration and death penalty/opioid crisis story, although the mainstream media generally treat these as two separate issues. But they are, in fact, closely connected, because illegal immigrants are much more likely to be involved in the drug smuggling trade than other population groups, as well as commit different violent crimes, because this is a younger population. Overall, illegal immigrants are more likely to be males 18-34, and this is a group that has a higher crime rate, including for trafficking drugs. So any effort to establish the death penalty for illegal drug smuggling has a direct impact on this illegal immigrant group.

Thus, it seems fitting to combine the blogs on these two topics into this single book. To this end, the book features chapters on these topics:

- how illegal immigrants really do commit more crimes,
- evidence from the Department of Justice showing that illegal immigrants have a higher crime rate than other groups,
- examples of some of the serious crimes committed by illegal immigrants,
- statistics showing that Hispanics commit more violent crime than whites,

- arguments disputing the liberals claim that the idea of the "criminal" immigrant is a myth,
- some suggestions for fixing the illegal immigration mess,
- why the death penalty is appropriate for opioid traffickers,
- how the death penalty can help to solve the national opioid crisis,
- how the death penalty works in other countries, such as Singapore and China,
- the case against the death penalty,
- some suggestions for dealing with the opioid crisis and the death penalty.

The book ends with an extensive Appendix, showing how the various statistical results and charts were derived.

Part I: The Illegal Immigration Problem

Chapter 1: Some Illegal Immigrants Really Do Commit More Crimes

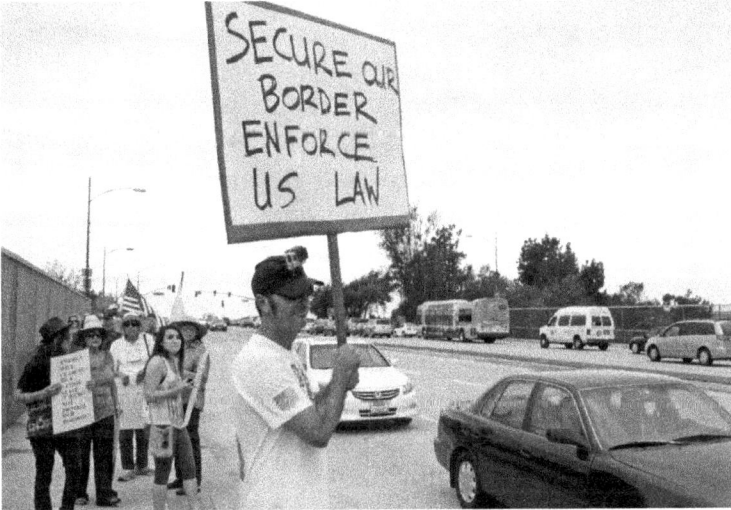

Citizens around the world are revolting against too much immigration. The revolt is especially profound in liberal Western Europe, where populism has reached a form of nationalism. The European Union itself could well become a casualty, as evidenced by Brexit, and increasingly anti-immigrant governments in previously Socialist countries. Each area has its own immigrant problem. The UK has to deal with immigrants from Eastern Europe. The near East has to deal with immigrants from Syria and Iraq. Europe has to deal with immigrants from there as well as Afghanistan and Africa. Bangladesh has to deal with immigrants from Myanmar. And we have to deal with immigrants from Mexico and Central America.

According to the national and mostly liberal U.S. media, immigrants commit less crimes. These statistics have been used to support an agenda that is designed to protect or provide citizenships for the Dreamers, the children of illegal immigrants, given a temporary reprieve on their immigration status over a series of two year extensions, so they could stay in the United States. These extensions continued for over a decade and were most recently extended under the Obama administration. President Trump rescinded the program as of March 5 and left it up to Congress to decide. But March 5 came and went without Congress being able to decide anything, and the courts weighed in to provide another six week extension while this issue was decided.

One of the central liberal arguments to support the Dreamers is that illegal immigrants are less likely to commit crimes. A similar argument has been used to support the illegals and prevent their deportation or any action by Federal agents to find and deport illegals. Liberals commonly refer to the illegals as "undocumented" immigrants, just as they have done in setting up so-called "Sanctuary" cities to protect them from being deported. But let's not use euphemisms; let's be clear that these immigrants are illegally here, and therefore they are rightfully being deported when they are discovered. So now let's concentrate on what we need to do deal with the illegal immigrants who should not be here, not the "Dreamers," as liberals like to call them, to evoke sympathy for the lives they have built in America.

Much of the argument of the liberals about the low rate of crime among the illegals is also false or misleading, if one looks more closely at the data. As it turns out, in some states and for some illegal demographic groups, the crime rate is actually higher for more serious crimes, such as robbery, theft, and crimes involving violence. This higher rate is particularly significant, since the illegals are more likely to come from this high-crime rate population, largely because illegals tend to come from a younger demographic from 16 to 35, which is more prone to crime than older groups. By contrast more settled immigrants are likely to have the lower crime rate frequently attributed to ALL illegal immigrants by the liberals to bolster their argument to keep the illegals here. Thus, a closer look at the data provides support for the government keeping illegals from coming into the U.S. and for being more selective about the immigrants that are permitted to come, such as immigrants who are older, more settled, and well-educated.

In fact, this more limited and selective approach is especially needed now, given that there are now over 65 million refugees around the world, and many of those let into other countries, such as about 1 million let into Germany, have already proved to be a problem for the police there. So just imagine if the U.S. had open doors and just a fraction of these 65 million refugees tried to gain refuge in the United States -- just 10% would be 6.5 million. Obviously that huge number of refugees admitted into the United States would be very destabilizing, given their problems with finding employment, poverty, differences in languages, and being drawn to crime, given a lack of other opportunities. Lately, the U.S. has allowed an average of about 1 million immigrants in a given year and never more than 2 million.

With those considerations in mind, let's look at some crime stats from Arizona.

A major study about illegal immigrants in Arizona found they had twice the crime rate as other residents, as described by Stephen Dinan in a *Washington Times* article: "Illegals Commit Crimes at Double the Rate of Native-Born: Study."[1] The report was issued by the Crime Prevention Research Center, and it used a previously untapped source of data from Arizona which examined criminal convictions. Among other things the study found that illegal immigrants between 15 and 35 represented less than 3% of the state's population, but they made up nearly 8% of its prison population. Moreover, the crimes they were convicted for were generally more serious than just being illegal immigrants. As the author of the report and president of the research center, John R. Lott Jr. pointed out, using the term "undocumented" to refer to illegal immigrants:

"There appears to be a huge difference between the two groups. The type of person who goes through the process to legally immigrate to the United States appears to be very

[1]Stephen Dinan, "Illegals Commit Crimes at Double the Rate of Native-Born: Study," *Washington Times*, January 26, 2018.
https://www.washingtontimes.com/news/2018/jan/26/illegals-commit-crimes-double-rate-native-born-stu/

law-abiding versus even the U.S.-born population. The reverse is true for undocumented immigrants -- they are committing crimes, and more serious crimes."

Lott also pointed out that among the nearly 4000 first and second-degree murder convictions, the distinction between the legal and illegal immigrants was huge. Whereas the legal immigrants represented less than 1% of the prisoners convicted of murder, the illegal immigrants represented nearly 13% -- much greater than their percentage of the prison population.

He also noted that illegal immigrants had five times the rate of convictions for money-laundering and kidnapping, and they were three times more likely to have convictions for drive-by-shootings.

Moreover, Lott emphasized that the crime-rate for illegal immigrants in the 18 to 35 year old group was especially significant, since many of the Dreamers are in this category and much of the current controversy is designed to gain support for them. He pointed out that the data from Arizona suggested that the illegals' crime rate was 250% higher than might be predicted by their percentage of the population.

In commenting on this report, Attorney General Sessions pointed out that the illegal immigrants were more likely to be convicted of sexual assault, robbery and driving under the influence. In fact, as he observed: "Tens of thousands of crimes have been committed in this country that would never have happened if our immigration laws were enforced and respected like they ought to be."

Not convinced? I'll have more to say about the relationship of immigration and crime in my next post, including some examples of serious crimes by illegal immigrants that haven't made the news. Certainly, we have plenty of crimes by legal residents -- too many crimes, as everyone would agree. But we don't need to have even more crimes committed by illegal immigrants, who, when the crime statistics are examined more closely, have now been shown to commit a disproportionate share of crimes. And certainly, if a study of statistics in Arizona could show such dramatic differences, it seems likely that similar studies in other states might reflect a similar pattern. Thus, it's important to look more closely at statistics to see some of the realities that may be hidden under the surface.

The next chapter features more stats on immigration and crime.

Chapter 2: Department of Justice Stats Show that Illegal Immigrants Commit More Crimes

Some newly released stats show that illegal immigrants really do commit more crimes, despite liberal claims that they commit less. That liberal claim may be true for older illegals who really are less likely to be criminals, just as crime declines generally for older populations. But the stats from the prisons which largely house younger criminals under 35, who commit most of the crimes, are deeply troubling.

This situation was described in a December 2017 discussion between news commentators Tucker Carlson and Mark Steyn, a conservative Canadian author, who now lives and works mainly in Woodside, New Hampshire. Steyn has written five books, including *America Alone: The End of the World as We Know It*, a *New York Times* bestseller.[2] As Steyn reported, according to the Department

---

[2] "Steyn: Truth on Illegal Immigrant Crime Was Hidden Due to Political Correctness," Insider, Fox News.com,

of Justice and Homeland Security Release Data on Incarcerated Aliens, 94% of all confirmed aliens in Department of Justice (DOJ) custody as of December 2017 were unlawfully in the United States. The vast majority of these illegal immigrants were there for drug related offenses.

Or more precisely, as Steyn described, there were 39,455 suspected or confirmed non-citizens in the custody of the Bureau of Prisons -- amounting to 21% of the total federal prison population. Of the total 37,557 immigrants in federal custody, 94% were illegal immigrants, primarily for drug smuggling offenses. Steyn further blasted the media and DOJ for keeping this information from the general public on the grounds of political correctness. In reality the lack of information from the media and DOJ permitted liberal support for the illegals who had made it into the U.S., and the illegals were more likely to vote for Democratic candidates. As Steyn put it:

> "These statistics, which for political correctness reasons we were prevented from knowing in recent years, show that this country is, in effect, importing a criminal class."

Moreover, Steyn stated that these figures "represent just the tip of the iceberg," because the vast majority -- approximately 90% -- of incarceration is at the state and local level, and the Department of Justice does not include that data in its report. However, I summarized similar crime data from Arizona in my previous blog. Moreover, the problem of immigrant gangs in major cities continues, and the majority of these gangs are made up of illegal immigrants, according to earlier DOJ reports[3] and recent statements supporting the DOJ's continued crackdown on both gangs and illegal immigrants.

---

http://insider.foxnews.com/2017/12/21/steyn-we-werent-told-truth-about-illegal-immigrant-crime-because-political-correctness

[3] Jessica M. Vaughan and Jon Feere, "Taking Back the Streets, ICE and Local Law Enforcement Target Immigrant Gangs," *Center for Immigration Studies*, September 30, 2008. https://cis.org/Taking-Back-Streets-ICE-and-Local-Law-Enforcement-Target-Immigrant-Gangs-0

The result in effect is that the U.S. is importing a criminal class, and why should it do so, since this is only adding to the criminal population, and "America has no shortage of citizens in the country who break the law."[4] In other words, why make America's already serious crime problem even worse by permitting illegals to come into and stay in the country, since they are more likely to commit crimes.

A Department of Justice report issued December 21, 2017 emphasized this point in its statement about the large number of immigrants coming to the United States and committing crimes. As Attorney General Sessions stated:

"At the border and in communities across America, our citizens are being victimized by illegal aliens who commit crimes. Nearly 95 percent of confirmed aliens in our federal prisons are here illegally. We know based on sentencing data that non-citizens commit a substantially disproportionate number of drug-related offenses, which contributes to our national drug abuse crisis. The simple fact is that any offense committed by a criminal alien is ultimately preventable. One victim is too many….We (have to) start welcoming the best and brightest while turning away drug dealers, gang members, and other criminals."[5]

One reason that the proportion of illegal immigrants is so high in federal prison is because immigrant offenses now account for about half of all federal prosecutions. Among these offenses are smuggling people into the United States. At the same time, illegal immigrants were convicted of offenses related to money laundering

---

[4] Ibid.
[5] "Department of Justice and Homeland Security Release Data on Incarcerated Aliens -- 94% of All Confirmed Aliens -- 94% of All Confirmed Aliens in DOJ Custody Are Unlawfully Present," December 21, 2017.
https://www.justice.gov/opa/pr/departments-justice-and-homeland-security-release-data-incarcerated-aliens-94-percent-all

and drugs at a higher rate than ordinary citizens along the southern border, due to drug trafficking activity by the Mexican cartels.

Certainly it is true that the vast majority of violent crimes, such as murder, assault, and rape, are prosecuted at the state and county level. And it is true that many of the offenses by illegal immigrants may be non-violent, such as smuggling individuals into the country or illegal entry to the country. But that does not negate the fact that illegals facilitate activities that are associated with a high rate of violence, such as drug trafficking, which is wreaking havoc as part of a national addiction crisis, especially in the inner cities.

Moreover, it is important to recognize that illegal immigrants have a very different demographic profile than natives, which contributes to the high crime rate when that rate is considered for a younger demographic than the population as a whole. As reported in a January 22, 2018 *National Review* article by Robert Verbruggen, "Re: Illegal Immigration and Crime," the Migration Policy Institute pointed out that illegal immigrants are concentrated in the 16-34 age range in which criminal behavior is most common. But while this criminal population group accounts for 26% of the native born, it accounts for 43% of the illegal immigrant population, so that means this is a group that has a much higher likelihood to commit crime -- about 60% higher than the native-born population.

As Verbruggen points out, the illegal immigrant population "should have a murder rate something like 60 percent higher than natural-born population, based on demographics alone." This greater propensity for crime in this younger population is borne out in the Arizona study, which shows that illegal immigrants in the 15-35 year old age range is "far more overrepresented among criminals, including murderers."

Thus, Verbruggen's conclusion firmly shows the dangers of allowing in illegal immigrants who are more likely to commit crimes than the general population, largely because they come from a younger demographic than the general population, and this younger population is more prone to crime. As he observes: "If young men are coming here, working for a few years, and going home, they're pumping up the U.S. crime rate simply by virtue of being young men." While these young men may work for a few years, this doesn't mean this is steady work, especially since illegals end up working in jobs involving physical labor that are generally short term projects, such as being hired for a construction crew for the key months for construction from about April through October, or being hired for a short-term harvest job for a few months in the fall. These are notoriously low-pay, hard labor job, which could readily lead illegal immigrants to seek out other sources of income, such as through property crimes like robbery and theft. Then, too, Verbruggen points out that among the native born, many nationalities with a high percentage of second and third-generation immigrants, particularly from Latin America, "have considerably higher rates than U.S.-born whites do." Moreover, as he emphasizes: "Illegal immigrants unquestionably have higher crime rates than legal immigrants do."

Accordingly, while illegals who manage to elude the justice system and become middle aged or old in America may have lower crime rates that depress the overall rates of comparing illegals and legal immigrants and native populations, it is important to recognize the contributions of the younger illegal immigrant population who make up the vast majority of illegal immigrants coming to the U.S. Liberals tend to point to the overall statistics in support of the illegal immigrants who have made it to the country. But that is really a whitewash of the true picture which requires looking at the statistics for the younger illegal immigrants.

A report from the Center for Immigration Studies: "Taking Back the Streets: ICE and Local Law Enforcement Target Immigrant Gangs," points to the growing danger of these gangs. As described in this report, since 2005, the Bureau of Immigration and Customs Enforcement (ICE) has arrested over 8000 gangsters comprising over 700 different gangs as part of their Operation Community Shield initiative. In particular, the immigrant gangs are singled out as an especially big threat to public safety since their members are prone to violence and involved in transnational gangs. As the article states:

> "The latest national gang threat assessment noted that Hispanic gang membership has been growing, especially in the Northeast and the South, and that areas with new immigrant populations are especially vulnerable to gang activity. A large share of the immigrant gangsters in the most notorious gangs such as Mara Salvatrucha (MS-13), Surenos-13, and 18th Street are illegal aliens."[6]

According to this report, the FBI estimates that there are about 30,000 violent street, motorcycle, and prison gangs, with about 800,000 members, with much of the growth in suburban and rural parts of the U.S. where criminal gang activity is relatively high. As of 2008, the FBI considered the gangs more violent, organized, and widespread than ever before, and this is a trend that has continued to grow. Most significantly, the crimes associated with gang activity, such as homicide, robbery, and aggravated assault, showed the greatest increases. At the same time, these gangs reflected an increase in the number and size of gangs made up of both legal and illegal immigrant youth, with about 75% coming from Mexico. Importantly, certain gangs, such as the MS-13 and 18th Street Gang, are composed of mostly illegal immigrants.[7]

To a great extent, these gangs are involved in the illegal drug trade. As the report states:

> "According to the National Drug Intelligence Center and other law enforcement sources, street gangs, along with outlaw motorcycle gangs and prison gangs, are the primary distributors of illegal drugs in the United States. Gangs increasingly are involved in smuggling large quantities of cocaine and marijuana and lesser quantities of heroin, methamphetamine, and MDMA (also known as 'ecstasy')

---

[6] Jessica M. Vaughan and Jon Feere, "Taking Back the Streets, ICE and Local Law Enforcement Target Immigrant Gangs," *Center for Immigration Studies*, September 30, 2008. https://cis.org/Taking-Back-Streets-ICE-and-Local-Law-Enforcement-Target-Immigrant-Gangs-0

[7] Ibid.

into the United States from foreign sources of supply and in the transportation of drugs throughout the country. Some street gangs and prison gangs have established relationships with Mexican drug trafficking organizations and these relationships have resulted in the evolution of many street gangs from retail-level distributors to smugglers."[8]

Since this report came out, the problem of immigrant gangs has continued, along with their continued involvement in the growing drug problem in the U.S. as expressed in statements by Attorney General Sessions. He has emphasized the need to continue to go after these gangs, as well as the effort generally to stop and reduce illegal immigration to the U.S.

So I rest my case. We have to look more carefully at these crime stats and immigration to sort out the real truth.

---

[8] Ibid.

Chapter 3: Some of the Serious Crimes Committed by Illegal Immigrants

   Probably the most well-known recent case involving an illegal immigrant and a violent crime involves the killing of Kate Steinle in San Francisco, when Jose Ines Garcia Zarate shot her on a pier with a stolen gun he claims he found there that went off accidentally. It is true that the jury bought his argument that this was an accident based on the bullet ricocheting on the ground before it killed her. But he was later found guilty of felony possession of a gun, whether he stole it or not. Had he been turned over by the San

Francisco Sheriff's Department to the Federal Immigration authorities, who would have deported him because of his extensive prior convictions and his repeated returns to the Bay Area, he would not have been on the pier, and Kate Steinle would not have been shot. In short, Kate Steinle's death is one that didn't have to happen, and it only happened because an illegal immigrant remained in the United States, rather than being deported, due to San Francisco sanctuary city policies, which remain in effect today.

The major media coverage of that one case also resulted in many other examples of immigrants committing serious crimes coming to light. They have been discussed in a few articles, but otherwise many of the violent crimes committed by illegal immigrants are generally not known to the larger American public. In turn, a review of these cases helps to support the argument for restricting immigration from illegal immigrants and increasing the number deported. Certainly, as liberals may argue in support of keeping illegal immigrants here, there are many similarly serious crimes committed by native born and legal immigrants. And that's true. There are. But that's not the point. What is important is that these are *additional* crimes by illegals that wouldn't have happened, if they weren't permitted to come to the United States or stay here.

Thus, one should consider their crimes as *additive*, rather than using statistics to compare the crime rates for illegals, non-illegal immigrants, and Native Americans. Comparisons are what liberals do in arguing that settled illegal immigrants commit less crime, or in suggesting that those illegals who commit more crimes largely come from a more crime prone younger generation from 15-35, just because more illegals come to the U.S. at a younger age. While all of these statistical arguments may be true, they avoid an essential rationale for reducing or eliminating the illegals in the country -- they represent an *addition* to the crimes committed by other populations.

With that context in mind, here are some examples of serious crimes committed by illegal immigrants to support my basic contention to keep them out or send them home, before they add any more crimes to the mix.

One of the most recent cases involved the death of an Indianapolis Colts football player Edwin Jackson and a Uber driver. They were both killed when a pickup truck driven at three times the speed limit by Guatemalan citizen Manuel Orrega Savala hit the car. The tragedy was even worse because Savala was in the country illegally and had already been deported twice, according to state police.[9] So this is one more *additive* crime committed by an illegal immigrant, regardless of the percentages in the comparative statistics.

Many more of these serious crimes by illegal immigrants can be found in the record of such crimes compiled by FAIR -- the Federation for American Immigration Reform.[10] Aside from a series of these crimes featured in an article "Examples of Serious Crimes by Illegal Aliens," FAIR has an archive of several dozen crimes committed in 2017, 2016, 2015 and even earlier. The site even has a series of "Stolen Life" videos featuring the lost lives of the individuals killed by illegal immigrants, as described by their family members who are still grieving for their loss.

I'll describe just some of these stories featured in Stolen Lives and then highlight some of the serious crimes profiled in the archives.

One of the most poignant stories is that of Ronald da Silva, who was shot and killed by an illegal immigrant, when da Silva was standing with a friend in his driveway on April 27, 2002. The killer had previously been deported, and he was sentenced to 21 years in prison. But one reason for featuring his story now is that he is scheduled to be released from prison in 2020, and in the video da Silva's mother, Agnes Gibboney, makes this powerful statement: "The guy that killed my son has a determinate sentence in prison, but I have a lifetime sentence of grief and pain." In response, she has been one of the ardent activists pushing for immigration reform.

---

[9] Pat Kessler, "Reality Check: Immigrants and Crime," BCS Minnesota, February 7, 2018. http://minnesota.cbslocal.com/2018/02/07/reality-check-immigrants-crime/

Another Stolen Life video features Tessa Tranchant's story. In this case, Tessa, 16, was sitting at a stoplight with her friend when Alfredo Ramos, an illegal immigrant from Mexico, rammed into her car on March 30, 2007. Ramos was drunk and speeding when he rear-ended her, and he had a history of prior convictions. But due to Virginia Beach's sanctuary policies, he hadn't been detained and deported. As a result of the accident, he was charged with two counts of involuntary manslaughter and sentenced to 40 years in prison.

In another rear-end accident, Sarah Root, 21, from Omaha, Nebraska, was killed on January 31, 2016, when Eswin Mejia, an illegal immigrant from Honduras who was street racing, plowed into her car. Sarah had just graduated from Bellevue University with a 4.0 GPA the day before she died. In this case, Mejia escaped any penalties, because this accident happened in Douglas County, Nebraska, which has sanctuary policies that interfered with local law enforcement's ability to cooperate with the U.S. Department of Homeland Security *Immigration* and Customs Enforcement (ICE) officers, who might have detained Mejia. Instead, he was allowed to post bail and get out of jail on a motor vehicular homicide charge. After his release he simply disappeared.

In another case described in the Stolen Lives series, Shayley Estest had obtained an order of protection against Igor Zubko, an illegal immigrant from Russia, 10 days before he killed her on July 24, 2015. Despite this order, Zubko entered her home and shot her. Though he entered the U.S. legally, he overstayed his visa, so he was in the U.S. illegally when he committed his crime. At least in this case, the police arrested him and charged him with first-degree murder.

Finally, to take one more example, Apolinar Altamiro, an illegal immigrant from Mexico, killed Grant Ronnebeck, 21, in Mesa, Arizona on January 22, 2015 when they had an argument about a pack of cigarettes while Ronnebeck was working at a convenience store. Altamirano was out on bond from a previous conviction, while ICE was deciding whether to deport him.

The archives also list a variety of crimes by illegal immigrants that range from assault and rape to murder, after excluding the cases involving human smuggling and importing drugs. For example, in 2017, some of the cases listed include these crimes:

- 15 years in prison for brutally torturing and abusing three small children,
- 50 years in prison for producing child pornography,
- 8 years in state prison and 5 years of probation for a child rape case,
- at least 18 years in prison for molesting a teenage girl an estimated 50 times,
- 20 years in prison for sexually assaulting and terrorizing a young woman,
- 20-29 years in prison for raping a 13 year old girl.

These are just a small fraction of the crimes listed for 2017, with many more for 2016, 2015, and in the older archives. I have left the prison sentences in to make another point: we taxpayers are paying for those prison stays.[11]

As previously noted, this is not to say that legal immigrants and native born Americans couldn't have committed any of these crimes. The point is that the crimes were committed by illegal immigrants, many who had returned after being initially deported or given sanctuary in cities or counties with sanctuary protections. So such cases add to the urgency of taking steps to better protect U.S. citizens from the crimes committed by illegal immigrants.

In Chapter 7, I'll suggest some solutions for providing this additional safety and security from illegal immigrants in the United States.

---

[11] See also Paul Brakke, *The Costly U.S. Prison System*, Preface, American Leadership Books, 2017.

Chapter 4: Hispanics Commit More Violent Crime than Whites

    While I have previously pointed out that blacks commit the most violent crimes[12], Hispanic still commit considerably more crimes than whites. Let me explain how I have reached this conclusion through a careful analysis of crime statistics.

    I first began to look at this crime data in my blog "All Lives Matter," where I pointed out that black-on-black killings per capita far exceeded black killings by police or whites. Although data on homicides of and by Hispanics are not available, violent crime statistics are available for blacks, whites and Hispanics,[13] so it is possible to show how the data illustrates the extent of violent crime committed by Hispanics.

---

[12] Paul Brakke, "All Lives Matter", American Leadership Books, blog, 2018.
[13] Rachel E. Morgan, "Race and Hispanic Origin of Victims and Offenders, 2012-15", U.S. Department of Justice, Bureau of Justice Statistics, Special Report, NCJ 250747.

As with any type of killing, violent crime victims and their offenders primarily occur within the same racial or ethnic group. Thus, white offenders are the main perpetrators of violent crimes against white victims; black offenders the main perpetrators of such crimes against black victims; and the same holds true for Hispanics. More specifically, where the racial or ethnicity of the offenders was known, 56.6% of the violent crimes against white victims were committed by white offenders, whereas only 14.7% of these crimes involved black offenders and 11.0% involved Hispanic offenders, while the racial and ethnic identity was not known in almost 20% of the cases for a variety of reasons. After ignoring that 20%, I'll show you how the crime rate for Hispanics is higher.

Between 2012 and 2015, the average number of whites, blacks, and Hispanic 12 or older in the U.S. was as follows:

Whites: 172,611,780
Blacks: 32,599,700
Hispanics: 41,364,400.

During the same time period, the victims of violent crime were as follows:

3,679,410 white victims annually
   56.6% committed by white offenders
   14.7% committed by black offenders
   11.0% committed by Hispanic offenders
   17.7% committed by persons of unknown race/ethnicity
850,720 black victims annually
   10.9% committed by white offenders
   63.2% committed by black offenders
   6.6% committed by Hispanic offenders
   19.3% committed by persons of unknown race/ethnicity
846,520 Hispanic victims annually
   20.0% committed by white offenders
   20.5% committed by black offenders
   40.3% committed by Hispanic offenders
   19.2% committed by persons of unknown race/ethnicity

If you are interested in seeing my step by step approach in conducting this analysis, that's in the APPENDIX.

Here's the final table from the APPENDIX, which shows victims and offenders of violent crime by race/ethnicity, based on the average for every 1000 potential offenders of each race or ethnicity.

	White victims	Black victims	Hispanic victims	All victims
White offenders	12.1	0.5	1.0	13.6
Black offenders	16.6	16.5	5.3	38.4
Hispanic offenders	9.8	1.4	8.2	19.4
All offenders[14]	--	--	--	--

The results couldn't be clearer. As the table indicates, per capita, blacks commit the most violent crime (38.4), while Hispanics commit only about half as much (19.4), but still considerably more than whites (13.6). Most significantly, this level of violent crime by Hispanic offenders is much higher than that of whites, since it contradicts the popular image of the low level of violent crime by Hispanics because of having a close-knit family and strong work ethic. Now all that may be true, but Hispanics -- particularly younger Hispanic males from 18-34 -- have a higher violent crime rate than whites, perhaps due to their greater involvement in the drug trade and in smuggling immigrants across the border, as mentioned in chapter 2.

The extent of Hispanic participation in violent crime is less well-known than that of blacks, and their relatively high rate of violent crime against mostly white and Hispanic victims is important new information for law enforcement and legislators to know how to deal with Hispanic perpetrators. This higher propensity for violence

---

[14] There are no values given in this row because the values within each column above cannot be added properly since they were normalized differently.

is also why there is a much higher percentage of Hispanics in prison than whites.[15]

This information about the criminality of Hispanics also puts the lie to the liberal contention that immigrants do not contribute to crime. Rather this data analysis indicates that Hispanics do commit more violent crime than whites, especially against both whites and other Hispanics. Moreover, it seems most likely that the Hispanics committing these violent crimes are illegal immigrants, since they commit more violent crime than Hispanics who are legal immigrants or long-established citizens. This is because a much higher percentage of illegal immigrants are in the 18-39 age group compared to the general population of Hispanic Americans, and this younger group commits far more violent crimes than other age groups.

The data analysis in the above table also shows that Hispanic offenders are even more likely to target whites than Hispanics, and that black offenders are equally prone to selecting white victims as black ones. These results present troubling news indeed for their potential white victims. Indeed, this analysis shows that whites have the highest rate of being victimized by all groups.[16] Much has been made of black-on-black and Hispanic-on-Hispanic crime, but these data suggest that the law-abiding white community has as much to fear from these minorities as it does from white criminals. No wonder white suburban housewives are especially fearful of falling victim to these groups.

Still, Hispanics have the most to fear from other Hispanics,[17] since illegal immigrants exhibit higher violent crime rates than other Hispanics (Chapters 1 and 2). As a result, law-abiding Hispanics

---

[15] Paul Brakke, *The Costly U.S. Prison System*, American Leadership Books, 2017.

[16] While it is not appropriate to compare results within a column or between columns from this table because different rows have been normalized differently, the first pie chart in the APPENDIX does show that there are more white victims of each class of offender than victims of any other race/ethnicity.

[17] See third pie chart or first table in APPENDIX.

should be encouraged to report illegals to the authorities in order to increase their own safety.

Blacks have the most to fear from members of their own group (16.5 per thousand and they should also be encouraged to cooperate more with authorities rather than blame them.

Chapter 5: The *Myth* of the Criminal Immigrant?

Liberals are trying to do virtually anything to show that immigrants do not increase crime, and that cities are really safer when immigrants move there. They even trotted out a new study from the Marshall Project,[18] to prove this contention. The study was featured on an Easter television report purporting to show that there is no correlation between the increase of immigrants in a very large number of individual U.S. cities and an increase in violent crime.[19]

The study argues that despite conservatives' claim that immigrants are violent criminals, the facts show this claim is a myth. However, the study is flawed because it fails to consider other data that undermine the conclusion which liberals have attempted to draw

---

[18] Anna Flagg, "The Myth of the Criminal Immigrant", The Marshall Project, 3/30/2018, https://www.themarshallproject.org/2018/03/30/the-myth-of-the-criminal-immigrant
[19] PBS NewsHour Weekend, 4/1/2018.

from it, as I discovered in analyzing the study. The criminal immigrant is no myth; it is true, as I will demonstrate.

First, let's look at the study, which has valid data for what it actually shows. This extensive study examined changes in both the immigrant population and violent crime in 200 U.S. cities from 1980 to 2016. The study surveyed both large and small cities all over the U.S. The data were gathered by a collaboration of investigators at four universities led by a sociologist at the State University of New York at Buffalo.

The most newsworthy conclusion of the study was that "in 136 metro areas, almost 70 percent of those studied, the immigrant population increased between 1980 and 2016 while crime stayed stable or fell." In the remaining metro areas, crime and immigration both increased, although even in these cities, immigration generally increased far more than crime.

I have no reason to doubt the data or the lack of correlation between increased immigration and violent crime. The results appear compelling, particularly since I use correlation analysis myself.[20] I know it is hazardous to assign causation when two factors in a study correlate with one another. For instance, a correlation may occur when two unrelated events happen coincidentally at the same time or when they both occur due to a prior event that causes them both. In neither case would it be correct to conclude that one of the two correlated events caused the other. On the other hand, an absence of correlation between two events can result in one incorrectly assuming that one thing does not cause another -- such as in this case concluding that immigration does not increase violent crime.

Liberals have based their conclusion that immigrants have a low crime rate based on the absence of a correlation showing an increase in crime when immigrants come to a city. However, other equally valid data demonstrate that crime increases for a certain subset of the immigrant population - namely younger illegal

---

[20] Paul Brakke, *The Costly U.S. Prison System*, American Leadership Books, 2017.

immigrants 18-35, who are more likely to be involved in crimes, particularly in drug trafficking.

So how did the liberals get it so wrong, since there are just a few ways that their conclusion would not be justified. One incorrect conclusion might arise if increases in immigrants occur but still be so small that they do not contribute significantly to violent crime. However, this is unlikely to be a factor, since violent crime actually *decreased* markedly in many cities over this time. Therefore, either the presence of more immigrants decreased crime or something else did.

That other possibility is that some other factors were much more important than immigration in causing the decrease in crime. Most importantly, violent crime decreased very significantly throughout the U.S. from 1980 to the present. This had nothing to do with more immigrants, legal or illegal, coming to a city. As to what caused this decrease in crime, there is no clear consensus among experts, although as discussed in previous blogs and books, it is likely that increased incarceration played a role in decreasing crime, particularly after 1992.[3,21] This might have been a major contributing factor by getting criminals of any age and background off the streets.

Accordingly, the most valid comparison would be to compare the violent crime rates in a city which increased its proportion of immigrants and the *same* city if it had not increased its immigrants. Unfortunately, this is not possible, since one can't compare a situation which already occurred with a situation which did not actually happen.

Another approach might be to compare crime rates between cities that had increased their proportion of immigrants and those cities that had not and look at the number of illegal immigrants in different age groups in the two sets of cities. This might show that the crime rate increased in the cities which had an increased growth in the younger illegal immigrants, as would be expected, given the

---

[21] The situation may have been different in the 1980s. Before crime rates had begun to decline in the 1990s, Flagg's own data suggest a possible close correlation between increases in immigrants and violent crime rates in the 1980s.

many studies that have shown an increase in crime in this age group. An influx of younger illegal immigrants might be expected to lead to an increase in certain types of crimes associated with this group, such as drug trafficking and murder and assaults due to gang wars. Unfortunately, the data on immigrant age may not be available. At the same time, any comparison between cities needs to take into consideration other factors that might affect the crime rates, because these rates vary so markedly from one city to another.

Thus, liberals are incorrect to claim that immigrants do not increase crime, since a lack of causation cannot be inferred from the correlation that they used. Rather, data show that illegals add to crime rates, if only because their younger age makes them more prone to crime.

Chapter 6: Some Suggestions for Fixing the Illegal Immigration Mess

In the previous articles in this series I discussed how the illegal immigrants commit more crimes, especially drug trafficking, and how the crimes they commit add to the crime problem already facing America. The younger more recent illegal immigrants are the prime offenders, since just by virtue of their youth, they are more likely to get involved in crime, as well as participate in the gang activity of the many gangs made up primarily of illegal immigrants, such as MS-13.

Therefore, something must be done to deal with this problem and find some solutions to both reduce illegal immigration and the crimes the illegal immigrants are involved with.

Following are my recommendations:

1. **Secure the border**. Even though liberals claim that there is a net migration back to Mexico, there are still bad hombres entering along with others illegals to improve their lives and those of

their families. An 1800 mile-long concrete wall may not be the answer, but some combination of walls, fences, greater patrols, drones, and more border security agents is. These different methods should all be used to provide additional security at the possible entry points for illegal immigrants. This border security should include having a check for passports or other entry documents at airports for international flights and highways from Mexico and Canada. These checks should incorporate additional checks on the validity of the documents provided, such as fingerprint checks or eye retina scans. Border security agents should tighten up the other ways that illegal immigrants might get into the country, such as by boats to the East and West Coast, tunnels from Mexico, and land journeys through the back country. While walls might work in some areas, illegals might still come through tunnels, rivers, or other natural points of entry, where the terrain doesn't permit walls. Accordingly, more efforts should be made to look for and block tunnels and use drones to look for parties of illegal immigrants trying to get into the United States by land or water.

2. **Discourage illegal immigration** by eliminating the access of illegal immigrants to most services provided by city, state, or local governments. This may even lead many such immigrants to leave the country voluntarily. This will also reduce the high cost of having to locate and deport millions of illegal immigrants, estimated to be about 11 million around the U.S. Such services might include drivers' licenses, health benefits, education, and the like. Should illegal immigrants already have access to benefits, these could be cancelled or they might be prevented from renewing their access, whichever policy is more efficient for the relevant agency.

3. **Monitor immigrant crime more closely.** Require the local and state criminal justice departments at all levels -- from the local police to the state attorney's journal office and courts -- to keep accurate records of all crimes, and include information to indicate whether the person arrested, tried, convicted, and sentenced to prison is a legal or illegal immigrant and from what country. Any

sentence meted out should also be recorded. These departments should also file a copy of these records each month with the Department of Justice, so the data for all of the jurisdictions and states can be combined to illustrate clearly the different types of crimes committed by both legal and illegal immigrants. This recommendation is being made since there is little local or state data available. The Department of Justice reports only provide detailed statistics for federal crimes and prisoners in federal prisons; but 90% of crimes are committed and processed at the local and state level. Only in this way will be have a clear picture of the extent to which illegal immigrants are involved in criminal activity across the country.

4. **Institute strict penalties and deportations for crimes committed by illegal immigrants.** These policies should be instituted both to promote public safety by getting illegals committing serious crimes off the street and a deterrent to potential criminals. In the event an illegal is arrested, he or should be subjected to a no-bail condition prior to a trial, and be given the option of leaving the country through self-deportation or risking harsh penalties as well as deportation if found guilty. Those deported due to criminal activity should be tagged with implantable microchips so that they can be more readily identified if they attempt re-entry to the U.S.

5. **Encourage the cooperation of community members to support the arrest or deportation of illegal immigrants engaged in criminal activity.** Community members who know of illegal immigrants often help to hide them or prevent their apprehension by the police or ICE. A community outreach program is recommended to provide further education and support, so community members will be more receptive to law enforcement professionals who are trying to find, arrest, and subject to deportation illegal immigrants involved in criminal activity. This outreach should be designed to help community leaders understand the value enforcement strategies provide to the community by making it safer. This outreach might

43

take the form of local forums and meetings in the homes of volunteers and block captains, much like crime prevention meetings.

6. **Limit the number of legal immigrants** to the United States each year to 500,000 and be more selective about the immigrants admitted. As a minimum, they should be able to pass a basic English test, and should have attained at least the equivalent of a high school education. They might also be given points for their achievements in school and professionally, and the immigrants with the highest scores would have the opportunity to participate in a drawing for who can come to the U.S. Points would be deducted for skills and occupations where there are sufficient numbers of qualified U.S. citizens. Provisional temporary work visa status could be provided for those occupations in high demand lacking sufficient numbers of qualified U.S. citizens, and the immigrants could earn points toward a subsequent drawing during their stay. In this way, only the best and brightest of the prospective immigrants would apply for the 500,000 spaces available each year. Family members and relatives might be given additional points because of their relationship, but then they would still have to qualify under the point system for entry. Consider making English the official language and requiring fluency in English before granting permanent residency green card status. This may reduce child education costs by limiting bilingual education and further discourage illegal immigration of families.

Part II: Using the Death Penalty for Opioid Traffickers

Chapter 7: Considering the Death Penalty to Solve Our National Opioid Crisis

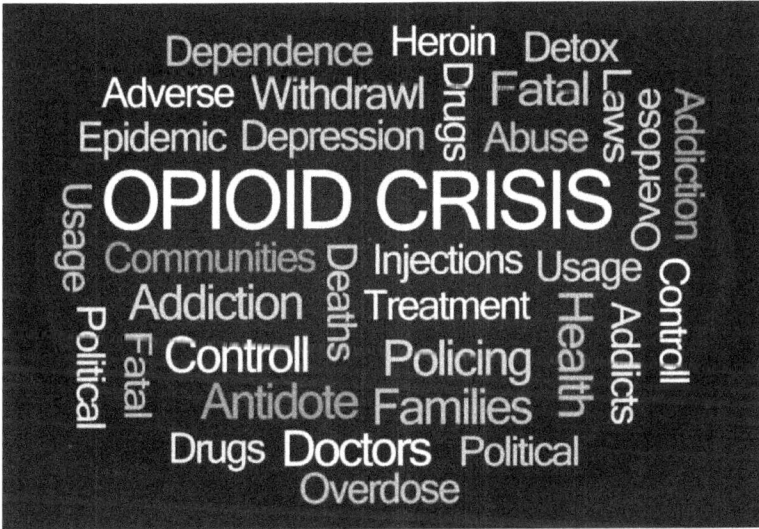

Today America is suffering from a drug crisis that has claimed hundreds of thousands of lives, affected millions more, and cost the economy many billions for the costs of interception, incarceration, medical treatment, and lost wages. The worst of the problem is due to opioids, including prescription pain killers, heroin, and synthetic derivatives of fentanyl.

The huge number of deaths due to drugs, as well as the high costs to the economy, certainly indicate the need to take action, including increased penalties. The President has even recently proposed the death penalty for dealing large quantities of drugs. Liberals are outraged by this proposal, but the President rightly points out that individual drug dealers are responsible for hundreds of overdose deaths, and we routinely demand the death penalty for mass homicides. The death penalty might well be a fit punishment, and possibly even a deterrent for future drug barons.

The High Cost of Drugs to Victims and the Economy

Before considering the remedies for drug addiction and the punishments for drug dealing, let's look at the stats showing the high costs for both drug victims and the economy. While liberals may propose just getting rid of the war on drugs and taxing drugs, they fail to look at the other side of the equation which involves holding the dealers complicit in the death of millions of victims of overdoses and addiction. They also ignore the high costs due to the many repercussions of drug use, including medical expenses, damages, and property losses from crimes committed by addicts to get money for drugs, and lost productivity.

So now let's consider these ravages to the economy.

- Over 50,000 Americans died of drug overdoses in 2015, over 33,000 from using opioids. Total drug overdoses soared to over 64,000 in 2016.[22] While opioids are legal when prescribed by a physician for a patient suffering from a serious illness or injury, the vast majority of victims have abused these drugs or obtained them illegally.[23]

- The opioid crisis costs the U.S. economy $504 billion, according to a report from the Council of Economic Advisers, an agency under the Executive Office of the President.[24] This includes the cost of treating overdoses, abuse, lost productivity, and costs incurred by the criminal justice system from the police, prosecutors, judges, and others involved in finding and arresting those involved in drugs, processing these cases and incarcerating those convicted. Aside from the financial costs, other costs include the spread of HIV/AIDS and Hepatitis C, deaths from overdose, effects on unborn

---

[22] "Drug War Statistics," Accessed 3/15/18.
http://www.drugpolicy.org/issues/drug-war-statistics
[23] Maria LeMagna, "The Opioid Epidemic Is Costing the U.S. More than $500 Billion Per Year," *MarketWatch,* March 11, 2018.
https://www.marketwatch.com/story/how-much-the-opioid-epidemic-costs-the-us-2017-10-27
[24] Ibid.

children, crime, unemployment, domestic abuse, divorce, and homelessness. [25]

- Heroin use is increasing, so that 600,000 people use it regularly.

- There is a relationship between age, sex and race. Nearly 40% of drug overdoses occur for those between the ages of 30 and 39. Because so many died young, in the past two years this has resulted tragically in the first decline in life expectancy in the U.S. Males and African Americans have higher rates of drug overdoses than others. [26]

- Data obtained from health agencies shows the ravages of the drug overdose epidemic, which is estimated to be even worse in 2017 than in 2016. Drug overdoses have become the leading cause of death among Americans under 50.[27]

- The opioid addiction crisis has become even more deadly as a result of an increase in illicitly manufactured fentanyl and similar drugs. Most of the time, fentanyl is sold on the street as heroin, or drug traffickers use it to make inexpensive counterfeit prescription opioids

- Because of the strength of fentanyl and its derivatives, the overdoses can be so severe, according to first responders, that giving victims multiple doses of naloxone, the anti-overdose medication sometimes called Narcan, doesn't work well anymore. Sometimes responders dose overdose victims with 12 to 14 or more hits of Narcan with no effect.[28]

- Currently, over 2 million Americans are at risk of dying from an overdose or addiction, since they are estimated to be

[25] Butt T., Reviewed the Richard N. Fogoros, M.D., "The Cost of Drug Use to Society," Verywellmind.com, January 10, 2018.
https://www.verywellmind.com/what-are-the-costs-of-drug-abuse-to-society-63037
[26] Ibid.
[27] Josh Katz, "Drug Deaths in America Are Rising Faster than Ever," *New York Times*, June 5, 2017.
https://www.nytimes.com/interactive/2017/06/05/upshot/opioid-epidemic-drug-overdose-deaths-are-rising-faster-than-ever.html
[28] Katz.

dependent on opioids, including heroin. These Americans come from all walks of life. For instance, in Deerfield Township near Akron, Ohio, the Narcotics Anonymous meetings include lawyers, accountants, and young adults and teenagers from middle-class parents.[29]

In short, the drug crisis in America is very real, with millions of victims, including hundreds of thousands of deaths, and billions of dollars in costs. Those who are producing and selling these drugs are the main perpetrators of this crisis. Drug dealers are not just responsible for the victims of overdoses or addictions, and the huge illicit profits from drug sales, but the high criminal justice costs in dealing with these cases, depending on how high up you go on the drug sales chain.

What to Do About the High Costs to Victims and Society

So why shouldn't such drug manufacturers, distributors, and sellers be penalized accordingly, and the more serious offenders be subject to the death penalty? Many others researching and writing about the drug crisis haven't considered the problem in these terms, when they instead talk about drug addiction being a diseases, discussing rehabilitation efforts, or dismantling the drug war because it has been so ineffective. These researchers and writers haven't thought in terms of viewing the bigger sellers as killers and upping the penalties accordingly. They should.

To this end, in the next chapters on dealing with the opioid crisis I will assess the merits of increasing the penalties, including the death penalty, for the worst criminals in the drug trade. I want to consider how we can learn from other countries that have implemented the death penalty successfully - Singapore and China, both of which have been cited by the President - to consider using the death penalty here in the U.S. to reduce the opioid crisis. These two chapters will make the case in favor of this use of the death penalty.

---

[29] Katz.

Chapter 8: Countries Using the Death Penalty for Drug Dealers: It Works in Singapore

   In the first article in this series, I described the ravages of an opioid crisis which is killing tens of thousands of victims each year. I also described some proposals to apply more stringent punishments, including the death penalty, to the dealers -- especially the higher-ups trafficking drugs.

   It's an approach that really works, as reflected in the success stories of applying the penalty in Singapore and China. This doesn't mean that the problem is entirely eradicated. But both countries have experienced marked declines in both drug trafficking and use, along with a decline in the kinds of crimes often associated with drug dealing, such as gang wars and drive-by shootings between rival gangs. You might consider these approaches used in other countries like pilot programs for implementing harsher penalties in the U.S. While there are already four types of capital punishment for drug-related crimes -- murder committed during a drug-related drive-by shooting, a murder committed with a firearm during a drug trafficking crime, a murder related to drug trafficking, and the death of a law-enforcement officer in a situation related to drugs -- these harsher penalties would apply capital punishment to drug trafficking itself, particularly to the leaders of trafficking organizations.

Thus, we have at least two good examples of other countries -- Singapore and China -- pursuing a crackdown to dry up the drug supply and hence the number of victims by using the death penalty for the most serious dealers. I'll feature the death penalty approach in Singapore in this post, and discuss the approach used in China in my next post.

The Death Penalty in Singapore

Singapore has had capital punishment since its days as a British colony, and this is one reason that Singapore prides itself as being a very safe country in which to live.

At one time, Singapore had the second-highest per-capita execution rate in the world -- from 1994 to 1998. In a survey taken in 2005, 95% of the population of Singapore believed in keeping the death penalty. In recent years the use of the penalty has declined, since only two people were executed in 2014, and no one in 2012 and 2013. This indicates that the approach has worked.

Singapore uses hanging to carry out its executions. However, Singapore lifted the mandatory death penalty for those convicted of drug trafficking or murder under certain circumstances, so the judge can sentence such offenders to life imprisonment, with the possibility of two appeals. Though rare, these appeals can be to a High Court Judge, the Court of Appeal, and finally to the President.

Singapore is particularly harsh on prisoners in drug cases in that 70% of the hangings have been for drug-related offenses. Under the penal code, just taking drugs into Singapore merits the death penalty, so this offense is right up there with various violent and very serious crimes, including waging or attempting to wage war against the government, piracy that endangers life, murder,

52

kidnapping, and robbery by five or more people that results in a death. In particular, under Schedule 2 of the Misuse of Drugs Act, this mandatory death sentence applies to anyone importing, exporting, or found in possession of more than the following:

- 1200 grams of opium and containing more than 30 grams of morphine
- 30 grams of morphine
- 15 grams of diamorphine (heroin)
- 30 grams of cocaine
- 500 grams of cannabis or 1000 grams of a cannabis mixture
- 250 grams of methamphetamine.

Plus there is a sentence for anyone manufacturing certain types of drugs including:

- morphine
- diamorphine (heroin)
- cocaine
- methamphetamine

It is also presumed, under the law, that any person with a controlled drug in his or her possession knows the nature of the drug.

These death penalty provisions seem to have been effective, in that according to some reports, Singapore has one of the lowest prevalence of drug abuse around the world. For instance, one blogger Benjamin Chang, reports that in over 20 years, the number of drug abusers arrested each year has declined from over 6000 in the early 1990s to about 2000 in 2011. There has also been a decline in the number executed for drug related crimes from the period when these executions were at a peak from 1994 to 2001, averaging about 20 to 40 executions a year. They dropped from zero to three each year during the period from 2007 to 2017.[30]

The government and its citizens believe that the policy has helped to keep Singaporeans safe. In the government view, the death penalty is only used in the most serious of crimes, including drug

---

[30] "Death Penalty Database," Cornell Center on the Death Penalty Worldwide, https://www.deathpenaltyworldwide.org/country-search-post.cfm?country=Singapore

offenses, which sends a strong message of deterrence to potential offenders. As stated by the Ministry of Home Affairs in January 2004 -- a position reaffirmed by the continuation of Singapore's death penalty policies: "The application of the death penalty is only reserved for 'very serious crimes… (the) death penalty has been effective in keeping Singapore one of the safest places in the world to work and live in." More recently, a similar statement about the effectiveness of the death penalty has been asserted by Vivian Balakrisknan, the Minister of Foreign Affairs, in a speech to the UN in September 2016. As she asserted: "In our view, capital punishment for drug-related offenses and for murder has been a key element in keeping Singapore drug free and keeping Singapore safe."[31]

Additionally, the success of combating drug abuse with the death penalty has inspired some American elected officials and office-seekers since 2012 to urge applying the Singaporean model in the U.S. For example, Michael Bloomberg, once a Mayor of New York City, said that the U.S. could learn from nations like Singapore's approach to drug trafficking in that "executing a handful of people saves thousands and thousands of lives." And Newt Gingrich, a high-profile Republican, has long advocated bringing Singaporean methods to support the U.S. War on Drugs.

Thus, this is one approach to dealing with drugs through capital punishment that definitely deserves consideration in the U.S. today. I'll discuss the approach used in China in the next chapter.

---

[31] "Singapore: Executions Continue in Flawed Attempt to Tackle Drug Crime, Despite Limited Reforms," *Amnesty International,* October 11, 2017. http://www.amnesty.org/en/latest/news/2017/singapore-executions-continue-in-flawed-attempt-to-tackle-drug-crime

Chapter 9: How China Is Using the Death Penalty for Drug Dealers: An Approach that Works

Like Singapore, China has had a long history of capital punishment as a legal penalty for murder and drug trafficking, though unlike Singapore, China uses lethal injection or a gunshot. China executes more prisoners than any other country each year, in part because it has such a large population.[32] Approximately 2400 were executed in 2016, a decline from a period in which China executed about 12,000 individuals in 2002[33], and 6500 in 2007[34].

---

[32] "Capital Punishment in China," *Wikipedia,* https://en.wikipedia.org/wiki/Capital_punishment_in_China

[33] Benjamin Haas, "Public Death Sentences for 10 People Show China's Desperation," *The Guardian*, December 19, 2017. https://www.theguardian.com/world/2017/dec/19/public-death-sentences-people-china-desperation

[34] "The Death Penalty in 2016: Facts and Figures," Amnesty International, April 11, 2017. https://www.amnesty.org/en/latest/news/2017/04/death-penalty-2016-facts-and-figures

China came to this resolve early during Chairman Mao's administration in 1949. China had an enormous opium addiction problem that had been inflicted on them by the British importing opium from India throughout the 19th century to both make profits and pacify the population. Two opium wars took place in this century, and the British prevailed, even gaining Hong Kong as a result of one of the wars. By 1906, there were 13.5 million opium addicts in China out of a total population of 400 million. Those 13.5 million addicts represented 27% of the adult male population. Now due to their crackdown on drugs, China has considerably reduced its opium problem. It has also gotten Hong Kong back, though Hong Kong is administered as an independent system, under Chinese laws.[35]

A major reason for the death penalty is to dissuade drug trafficking, and the public nature of these executions shows China's commitment to this policy, which has gained widespread public support. For example, in December 2017, thousands of observers watched as 10 people were sentenced to death in a sports stadium in Lufeng in the southern Guangdong providence, about 100 miles from Hong Kong. Of the 10 executed, seven were convicted of drug-related crimes, while the other prisoners were found guilty of murder and robbery.[36]

To put on this spectacle, local residents received an official notice through the social media inviting them to attend the sentencing. As the crowd watched, a police truck with its blaring sirens arrived with the accused, who were each surrounded by four officers wearing sunglasses. Then, one by one, the accused were escorted to a small platform to hear their sentences read. After that, they were whisked away to be executed. Five months earlier, eight offenders were sentenced to death for drug crimes in a similar way.

---

[35] "Opium in China," *Facts and Details,*
http://factsanddetails.com/china/cat11/sub74/item139.html
[36]Benjamin Haas, "Thousands in China Watch as 10 People Sentenced to Death in Sport Stadium," *The Guardian,* December 17, 2017.
https://www.theguardian.com/world/2017/dec/18/thousands-china-watch-executed-sport-stadium

Such open air sentencing is staged as part of China's drug crackdown, where drug dealers are treated much like terrorists.

While such sentences are meted out as the result of a series of formal criminal proceedings, it is also a system where the prosecutor almost always wins when a case is brought to trial, since prosecutors have a 99.9% conviction rate.[37] While China has a two or three step appeals process, in about 85% of appeals, the original verdict is confirmed. Should the judges uphold the death sentence, the defendant is soon executed.

However, offenders who are under 18 at the time of the crime cannot be given the death penalty.

These policies and procedures, in turn, provide some insights into how a death penalty case might be prosecuted in cracking down on drug offenders in the United States. For example, offenders might expect to receive a death penalty sentence if there is ample evidence to show their high level of involvement in drug trafficking, which might contribute to them providing information to arrest and convict those even higher up in their criminal organization in exchange for a more lenient sentence.

In sum, there is much we can learn about instituting a death penalty for drug trafficking in the United States, as well as in showing that the policy has widespread support, such as in having a public sentencing ceremony as has been conducted increasingly in China.

---

[37] Ibid.

Chapter 10: The Case against the Death Penalty as a Fix for Our Drug Problems

The previous three chapters in this section of the book have entertained the suggestion by the President that the death penalty should be imposed on drug traffickers who have caused the overdose deaths of numerous addicts. Consequently, we know that the opioid crisis is extremely severe, and that it has been "tamed" in Singapore and China to a great extent by their institution of the death penalty for drug traffickers. So would a similar measure work here? After all, the U.S. applies the death penalty on many crimes, including murder, terrorism, and treason.

In many ways, our society is not like those in Singapore or China. To be effective, China uses public sentencing to strengthen the deterrent. That might not go over as well in the U.S. Singapore has used extensive top-down authority to keep its many ethnic groups in check and to guard against offenses to the public order, even gum chewing, which are the kinds of things that states' rights groups in the U.S. would find offensive. But the biggest cultural difference is that Asian societies value their elders more than we do and are more willing to do as they are told. Besides, U.S. liberals are not inclined to defer to the President on matters where they disagree.

These Asian countries probably don't have as many violent foreign drug traffickers as we do. Given the lucrative profits inherent in the drug trade, it is hard to imagine drug kingpins and gangs in Mexico, Central America and Colombia being deterred by the threat of a death penalty. In fact, these gangs are known for violence, which has resulted in tens of thousands of deaths in these turf battles. And some cartel leaders have been able to hide away for years to rule their gangs, and a few have managed to live like kings in their "prisons" or have gotten accomplices outside to help them engineer elaborate escapes, such as El Chapo did as one of the biggest Mexican drug lords.

What else would need to be taken into consideration? Here are some slippery slope issues:

- Where do you draw the line? Should the death penalty be imposed on those who have sold X number of grams of heroin in a certain period of time or those who have supplied the heroin that resulted in Y number of cases of heroin overdose? And how would these numbers be determined? Whatever numbers are set for the penalties to kick in would have to be substantiated in a court of law. How would we translate grams of heroin to milligrams of fentanyl? Would a small time dealer who had been given a bad batch of fentanyl-laced "heroin" be more liable than the bigger dealer who supplied him? If he had checked out the product personally, he'd probably be dead. Many lower level dealers or smugglers act more as conduits or "mules" who sell or transport what they have been given without checking the merchandise. How guilty should they be, given their lack of knowledge of the potency or value of what they are transporting?

- What about prescription painkillers? There is little doubt these started our national crisis, since opioids were responsible for 42,249 deaths in 2016 according to the Center for Disease Control and Prevention, [38] and 63,600 deaths that year according to the National Center for Health Statistics. [39] So it's no wonder that there is a sense of crisis about these drugs leading to a major cause of death. Yet relatively few deaths result directly from unintentional overdoses of prescription painkillers. We are certainly right to limit their use, but it seems excessive to impose the death penalty for prescribing physicians or the companies that manufacture them, since these drugs have their legal uses and save millions from debilitating pain or death. Shouldn't the real culprits be the individuals who abuse them or the drug dealers who provide these pills through illicit channels to users and abusers?

- What about other illegal drugs? Methamphetamine might well fall into the same category of causing deaths, although not as many (only 7663 in 2016, according to the "Overdose Death Rates" report from the National Institute for Drug Abuse).[40] Personally, I would contend it should be in the same category as the opioids. But what about PCP or ecstasy? These may cause violent behavior but probably not as many deaths. What about cocaine? Overdoses due to

---

[38] "Drug Overdose Death Data," Centers for Disease Control and Prevention," https://www.cdc.gov/drugoverdose/data/statedeaths.html
[39] Holly Hedegaard, M.D., Margaret Warner, Ph.D., and Arialdi M. Miniño, M.P.H., "Drug Overdose Deaths in the United States, 1999–2016," NCHS Data Brief, No. 294, December 2017. .https://www.cdc.gov/nchs/data/databriefs/db294.pdf
[40] "Overdose Death Rates," National Institute for Drug Abuse, September 2017. https://www.drugabuse.gov/related-topics/trends-statistics/overdose-death-rates

cocaine totaled 10,619 in 2016.[41]   Crack cocaine devastated the black community some number of years ago, then subsided, but overdoses due to cocaine are on the rise again more recently.[42] We should be more selective in determining which drugs are the most responsible for causing a large number of deaths, and then limit the death penalty to dealers of those drugs.

- What about marijuana? There are very few reported cases of death by marijuana overdose. It is not even as dangerous to adults as alcohol. And now marijuana is legal medicinally in 30 states, and recreationally in 8 of those. The President recently even assured Colorado Senator Cory Gardner that he would consider marijuana usage a states' rights issue rather than a federal one, which would protect marijuana usage where it has been legalized.[43] A majority of Americans (61-64%, including 51% of Republicans according to polls by the Pew Research Center and *Forbes*)[44] favor its legalization. Under the circumstances, it would be hard to imagine making the death penalty applicable to marijuana dealers.

- What about alcohol? We've been there before with Prohibition. Too bad that didn't work, because alcohol

---

[41] Ibid.

[42] Ibid. https://www.drugabuse.gov/related-topics/trends-statistics/overdose-death-rates

[43] "Got Pot Pledge from Trump, Senator Says," *Arkansas Democrat-Gazette*, 4/14/2018.

[44] Abigail Geiger, "About Six-in-Ten Americans Support Marijuana Legalization," FactTank, News in the Numbers, Pew Research Center, January 5, 2018. http://www.pewresearch.org/fact-tank/2018/01/05/americans-support-marijuana-legalization; Tom Angell, "Poll: Legal Marijuana Support at Record High in U.S.," October 25, 2017, Washington: Beltway Brief, Forbes.com https://www.forbes.com/sites/tomangell/2017/10/25/poll-legal-marijuana-support-at-record-high-in-u-s/#1ffd807843ff

probably costs even more to society than the opioid crisis, including lots of violence and deaths. The President knows this all too well, having lost his brother to alcohol addiction. Wisely, he just says no, but most Americans don't seem to be able to follow suit. The death penalty won't work for alcohol. There are too many millions of users.

- What about tobacco? It causes even more deaths than alcohol. The deaths are much more delayed and chronic and have cost the health of sufferers and the healthcare system a fortune. Unfortunately tobacco is still legal; otherwise cigarette manufacturing executives who deceived the public for years would be prime candidates for death penalty consideration.

As you can see, there are numerous practical considerations that would make the death penalty idea problematic to implement. The President deserves credit for politically incorrect outside-the-box thinking on this critical issue, and I agree that many opioid traffickers deserve the death penalty, but I am afraid that a greater emphasis on the other aspects of his proposed fixes for the opioid crisis is probably in order.

One last point. Arkansas ranks second only to Alabama in terms of states prescribing the most opioids and in opioid abuse by young people.[45] Mr. President, why didn't you come here to announce your opioid policy rather than New Hampshire, which you narrowly lost in 2016? We gave you a 26.6% margin of victory against Hillary, and we certainly would have given you a warmer reception than freezing New Hampshire. For that matter, so would West Virginia or Alabama, states with just as big opioid problems that gave you even larger margins of victory.

---

[45] Amanda Claire Curcio, "State, Cities, Counties Sue Opioid Makers, Suppliers," *Arkansas Democrat-Gazette*, 3/22/2018.

Chapter 11: Some Suggestions for Dealing with the Opioid Crisis

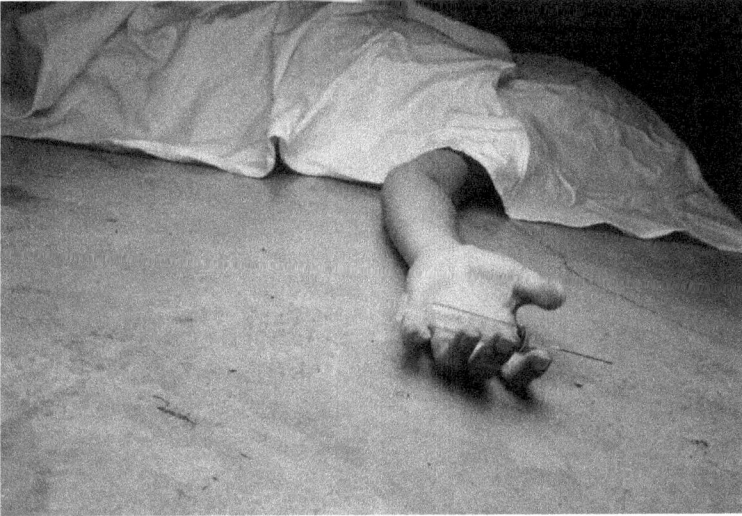

In the previous chapter in this series, I discussed the President's suggestion that the death penalty should be imposed on drug traffickers, why it is justified, and yet how its implementation would create severe practical difficulties. If not this approach, what other strategies should be pursued? Alas, there is no one simple fix, so several different strategies need to be pursued simultaneously.

The President recommended mandatory minimum sentencing as a penalty for distributing certain opioids, and this recommendation has been seconded by Senator Tom Cotton of Arkansas, with sentencing duration dictated by the amount of substance seized. This crackdown may help reduce supply, but it will need to be supplemented with greater interdiction efforts at all ports of entry and along our borders. Another reason for greater border security!

The President also recommended expanding access to *proven* treatment and recovery efforts. This recommendation is primarily aimed at reducing demand rather than supply. There are many treatment centers and plans, some more effective than others. Once the best strategies are determined, such treatments should be carried out on a mandatory basis on addicts in prisons and jails, even if that requires segregated facilities for them. Otherwise, they will easily relapse once released and revert back to a life of crime to feed their habit. Different treatment plans could be tried out on prison populations in order to determine which are the most effective. Sentences could be reduced for those who "come clean," by both stopping use and identifying their own suppliers.

Finally, the President recommended broadening awareness and education of the crisis. By now it is likely that most adult Americans are familiar with the crisis, which suggests that adolescent youth and their parents should be targeted. An educational campaign in all schools, including a series of videos about the dangers of addiction, deaths due to drugs, and the crackdown on drug dealers, might help reduce the influence of adolescent peer pressure. Videos should also be produced for parents advising them what to be on the lookout for and giving them advice on dealing with their adolescent children on this issue.

Although all three of these sets of recommendations in the President's plan have been proposed previously and represent more conventional approaches than the death penalty, they are all worthwhile, and the President must be complimented on putting them forth and implementing them with actual spending. Kudos to the President.

Following are some additional suggestions of my own:

1. **Create a separate drug sales court to deal with death penalty for drugs trafficking cases.** This approach will help to streamline the justice process by putting these cases in a separate track in the court system. Also, this separate track will enable these cases to be heard by a drug sales court judge, rather than being heard by a jury. This judge will be more knowledgeable and less likely to

be moved by emotion or the political controversy that can be associated with these cases. This streamlining will also cut down the cost and length of time of dealing with these cases. No bail should be permitted for alleged opioid traffickers.

2. **Set up a separate division in the prisons or separate prison wings to house drug traffickers.** This separation will contribute to making the prisons more efficient and cost-effective through isolating drug traffickers. This isolation of the traffickers will also provide better monitoring of the visitors to those prisoners, since they might still be involved in drug trafficking. Additionally, this separate treatment for dealers will put their visitors on notice of the risks of remaining involved, and therefore contribute to their leaving the drug trade, too.

3. **Publicize the names of the individuals sentenced under the new laws.** This notification will help to remind the members of the community of the penalties for dealing drugs and discourage their own involvement.

4. **Set up a tip line for information that leads to the arrest of drug traffickers**. This tip line can be set up so that callers can protect their anonymity, as well as claim substantial rewards by providing information that leads to the arrest of high-level drug dealers who are subject to the death penalty. These rewards can be tiered, so that those who target higher-level drug dealers can earn more, and an encrypted system can be set up so that tipsters can both remain anonymous yet claim a reward.

5. **Provide more funds for research into better addiction treatments**. As mentioned previously, the President wishes to increase access to *proven* treatment programs. Present treatments are only moderately effective and relapse occurs frequently. More effective treatments are sorely needed. The opioid epidemic is every bit as critical as the HIV/AIDS epidemic was, and yet addiction research receives only a fraction of the funds that AIDS research

did. Opioid users are not able to mount the kind of concerted lobbying effort that homosexuals managed, because they are debilitated by their addiction, and the families of opioid users have not been able to lobby for them either, since often addicts are estranged from their families. Thus, providing assistance with researching treatment options is one arena where the federal government has to intervene.

In making these recommendations, I acknowledge that I am a researcher at a biomedical institution, but I suggest these strategies solely as a concerned citizen. My own research has nothing to do with addiction.

Appendix

This Appendix features the methods used to obtain the conclusions of the data analysis presented in Chapter 4.

First up are the numbers introduced at the beginning of Chapter 4. To begin, we have to calculate the number of white victims of offenders of each race or ethnicity. Of the average ~~of~~ 3,679,410 ~~of~~ white victims annually, 56.6% of them represent the 2,082,546 whites who were victimized by whites, 14.7% of them (540,873) were victimized by black offenders, and 11% (404,735) were victimized by Hispanic offenders (as shown on the pie chart below).

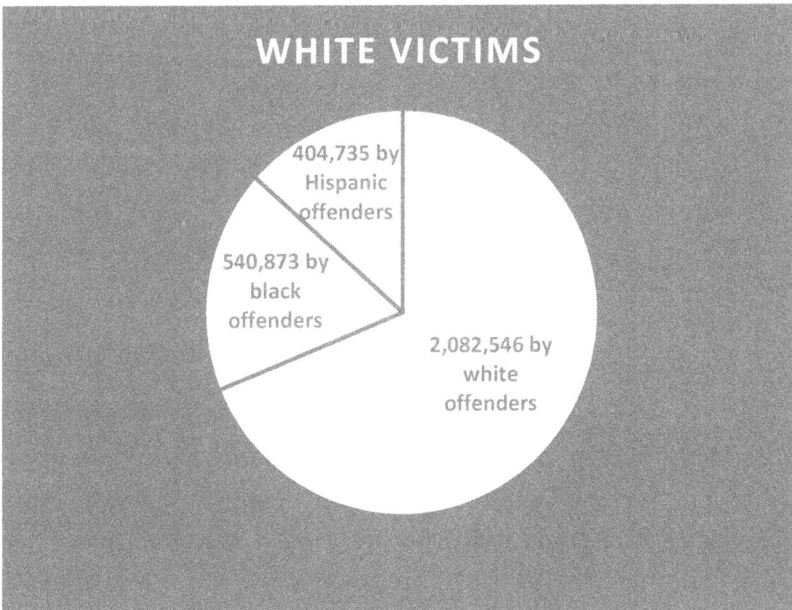

WHITE VICTIMS

404,735 by Hispanic offenders

540,873 by black offenders

2,082,546 by white offenders

The second step is to normalize (divide) these numbers by the total number of whites and the race/ethnicity of the victims and express the result per 1000 victims. This is shown in the upper portion of the bar graph below, which simply represents another way to demonstrate which race or ethnicity victimized the most whites.

White victims per thousand of race/ethnicity of victim or offender

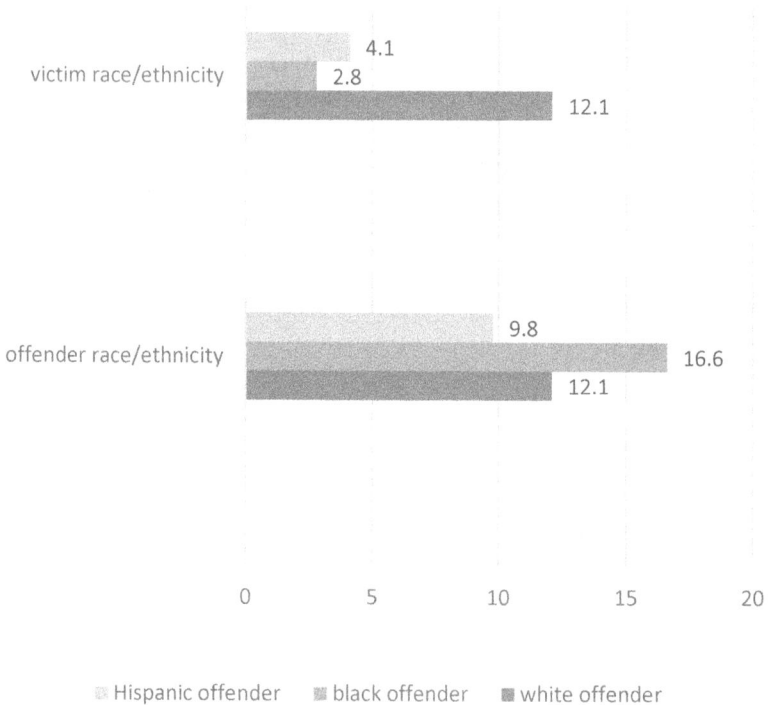

victim race/ethnicity
- 4.1
- 2.8
- 12.1

offender race/ethnicity
- 9.8
- 16.6
- 12.1

| | 0 | 5 | 10 | 15 | 20 |

Hispanic offender   black offender   white offender

The third step is to normalize these numbers instead by the total number of whites, blacks or Hispanics to represent the race/ethnicity of the offenders. Since there were 172,611,780 whites as possible offenders, this works out to be (2,082,546 ÷ 172,611,780) x 1000 = 12.1 white victims per thousand whites (lower bar graph above). By the same reasoning 540,873 whites were victimized by some of the 32,599,700 blacks, or 16.6 white victims per thousand blacks, and 404,735 whites were victimized by some of the 41,364,400 Hispanics, or 9.8 white victims per thousand Hispanics.

Next we'll use the same three steps to deal with black victims. For the first step, there were an average number of 850,720 black victims annually, and 10.9% of them (92,728) were victimized by whites, 63.2% (537,655) by blacks, and 6.6% (56,148)

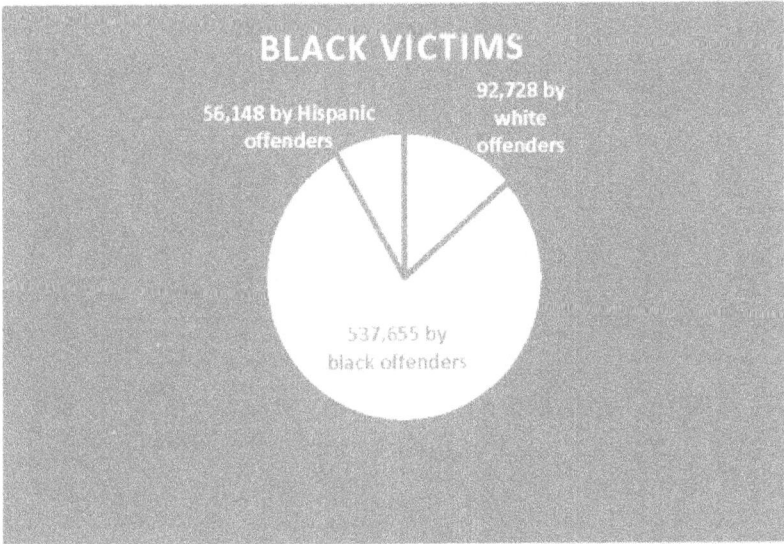

BLACK VICTIMS

56,148 by Hispanic offenders

92,728 by white offenders

537,655 by black offenders

In the second step, we normalize (divide) these numbers by 32,599,700, the total number of blacks to determine the rate per thousand based on the race/ethnicity of these victims. This is shown in the upper portion of the bar graph, which simply represents another way to demonstrate which race or ethnicity victimized the most blacks.

In the third step, we normalize these numbers instead by the total number of whites, blacks or Hispanics to determine the rate per thousand based on the race/ethnicity of the offenders. Since there were 32,599,700 blacks as possible offenders, this works out to be (92,728 ÷ 172,611,780) x 1000 = 0.5 black victims per thousand whites (as shown on the lower bar graph). By the same reasoning 537,655 blacks were victimized by some of the 32,599,700 blacks, or <u>16.5 black victims per thousand blacks</u>, and 56,148 blacks were victimized by some of the 41,364,400 Hispanics, or <u>1.4 black victims per thousand Hispanics</u>.

Black victims per thousand of race/ethnicity of victims or offenders

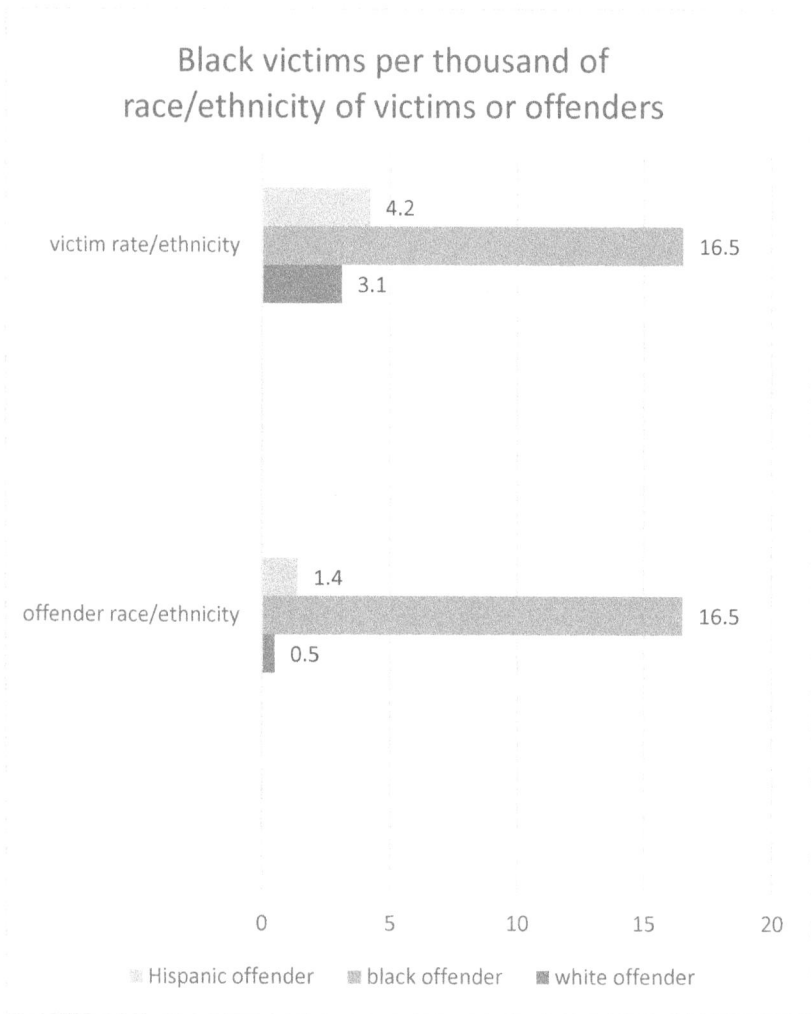

Now let's look at the rate of victimization of Hispanics. There were an average number of 846,520 Hispanic victims annually, 20.0% (169,304) of whom were victims of whites, 20.5% (173,537) of whom were victims of blacks, and 40.3% (341,148) of whom were victims of Hispanics (as indicated on the pie chart below.

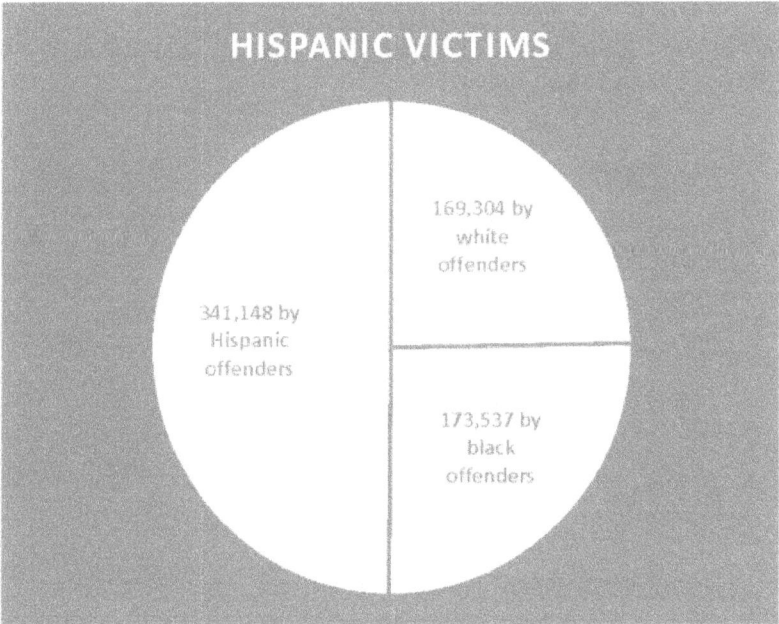

HISPANIC VICTIMS

169,304 by white offenders

341,148 by Hispanic offenders

173,537 by black offenders

Second, we normalize (divide) these numbers by 41,364,400, the total number of Hispanics, the race/ethnicity of these victims, as shown in the upper portion of the bar graph below, which simply represents another way to demonstrate which race or ethnicity victimized the most Hispanics.

Third, we normalize these numbers instead by the total number of whites, blacks or Hispanics to represent the race/ethnicity of the offenders. Since there were 172,611,780 whites as possible offenders, this works out to be (169,304 ÷ 172,611,780) x 1000 = 1.0 Hispanic victims per thousand whites (lower bar graph). By the same reasoning 173,537 Hispanics were victimized by some of the 32,599,700 blacks, or 5.3 Hispanic victims per thousand blacks, and 341,148 Hispanics were victimized by some of the 41,364,400 Hispanics, or 8.2 Hispanic victims per thousand Hispanics, as shown in the lower bar graph below.

Hispanic victims per thousand of
race/ethnicity of victims or offenders

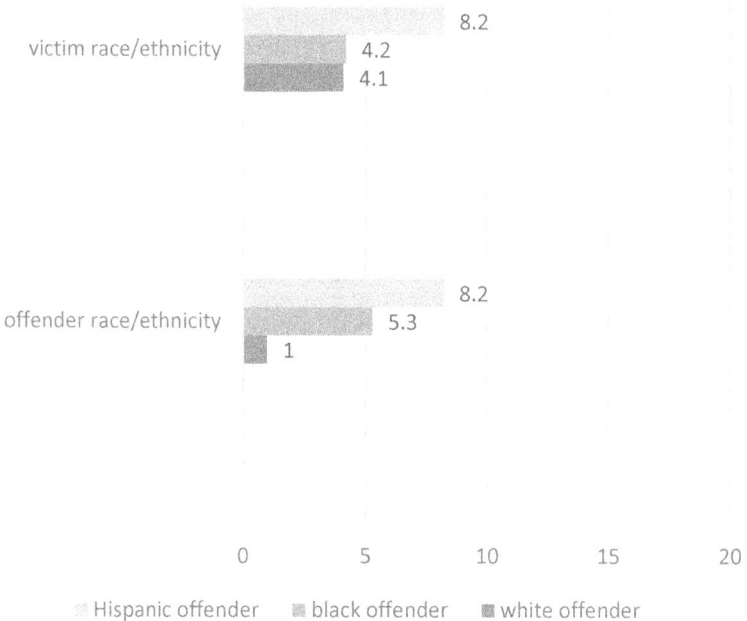

victim race/ethnicity
8.2
4.2
4.1

offender race/ethnicity
8.2
5.3
1

0   5   10   15   20

Hispanic offender   black offender   white offender

The next step is to take these numbers and incorporate them into two tables. The first table shows the numbers from the three sets of upper bar graphs, obtained by dividing by the race or ethnicity of victims.

	White victims	Black victims	Hispanic victims	All victims[46]
White offenders	12.1	2.8	4.1	--
Black offenders	3.1	16.5	4.2	--
Hispanic offenders	2.3	1.7	8.2	--
All offenders[47]	21.3	26.1	20.5	--

An analysis of the numbers in the table reveals the following: Examining columns, it is clear that whites are most likely to be victimized by whites (12.1), blacks by blacks (16.5), and Hispanics by Hispanics (8.2). In making these comparisons, only the numbers within a column have been compared, since they are all normalized by the same factor, the race/ethnicity population of those victims.

It is not appropriate to make comparisons along rows or between rows because the normalization is different for each entry, rather like comparing apples and oranges.

Other comparisons may be drawn from a second table constructed from the numbers generated by the lower set of bar graphs in this Appendix.

The following table shows the rates for the different types of offenders and their victims, but in this case the numbers are instead

---

[46] There are no numbers in this column because the rows to the left are not additive (they are each divided by different numbers for victims' populations).
[47] The numbers in this row are larger than the sum of the columns above because they include the nearly 20% of victims whose offenders' race/ethnicity could not be determined.

normalized by the population of the race/ethnicity of the offender. This makes comparisons along rows appropriate, although not comparisons within columns. These comparisons have generated the analyses spelled out in Chapter 4.

	White victims	Black victims	Hispanic victims	All victims
White offenders	12.1	0.5	1.0	13.6
Black offenders	16.6	16.5	5.3	38.4
Hispanic offenders	9.8	1.4	8.2	19.4
All offenders[48]	--	--	--	--

---

[48] There are no values given in this row because the values within each column above cannot be added properly since they were normalized differently.

About The Author

Paul Brakke is a research scientist based in central Arkansas. He became interested in the criminal justice system because, as described in his first book *American Justice?,* his life was turned upside down by the system. This occurred after his wife was falsely accused of aggravated assault for trying to run over a 12-year old boy with her car. A group of kids and some neighbors wanted her out of the neighborhood. Eventually, the Brakkes were forced to move as part of a plea agreement, since otherwise, Brakke's wife was threatened with a possible 16-year jail sentence if the case went to trial and she lost.

After an initial critique of the criminal justice system, he went on to look at other problems in the system and the country in general and how to fix them. His other books now include: *The Price of Justice, Cops Aren't Such Bad Guys, The Great National Divides, Fixing the U.S. Criminal Justice System,* and *The Costly U.S. Prison System.*

Now he has added this book. Over the past four years, he has become an expert on the criminal justice system and has become a speaker and consultant on this topic. He has also set up a publishing company American Leadership Books, featuring books on criminal justice and social issues which are available in print and e-books through Amazon, Ingram, Kindle, and other major distributors.

The books' websites are www.americanleadershipbooks.com and www.americanjusticethebook.com.

Other Available Books

American Justice?

The Price of Justice in America

Cops Aren't Such Bad Guys

The Great National Divides

The Great National Divides (in Full Color)

Fixing the U.S. Criminal Justice System

The Costly U.S. Prison System (in Full Color)

Contact Us

For more information:

AMERICAN LEADERSHIP BOOKS
Little Rock, Arkansas
(501) 503-8614
brakkep@gmail.com

www.ingramcontent.com/pod-product-compliance
Lightning Source LLC
Chambersburg PA
CBHW071246020426
42333CB00015B/1656